This BLOOMSBURY Activity
Book belongs to:

_____

BLOOMSBURY
Activity Books

Away in a manger

Away in a manger
    no crib for a bed,
The little Lord Jesus
    laid down his sweet head.
The stars in the bright sky
    look down where he lay,
The little Lord Jesus
    asleep on the hay.

The cattle are lowing,
    the baby awakes,
But little Lord Jesus
    no crying he makes.
l love thee, lord Jesus;
    look down from the sky,
And stay by my side
    until morning is nigh.

Be near me Lord Jesus
    l ask thee to stay,
Close by me for ever
    and love me, l pray.
Bless all the dear children
    in thy tender care,
And fit us for heaven,
    to live with thee there.

F(D)

stars in the ___ bright sky looked

D7(B7)

down where he lay,

Gm(Em)

The ___

C7(A7)

lit - tle Lord

F(D)

Je - sus a -

Gm(Em) C(A) F(D)

sleep on the hay.

Activity: Add more
sticker owls to the
branches.

Angels from the realms of glory

Angels from the realms of glory,
Wing your flight o'er all the earth;
Ye who sang creation's story
Now proclaim Messiah's birth;
    Gloria in excelsis Deo,
    Gloria in excelsis Deo.

Shepherds in the field abiding.
Watching o'ver your flocks by night,
God, with man is now residing,
Yonder shines the Infant Light:
    Gloria in excelsis Deo,
    Gloria in excelsis Deo.

Sages, leave your contemplations;
Brighter visions beam afar.
Seek the great desire of nations;
Ye have seen his natal star:
    Gloria in excelsis Deo,
    Gloria in excelsis Deo.

Activity: Which angel is the odd one out?

Ding dong merrily on high

Ding dong merrily on high!
In heav'n the bells are ringing.
Ding dong verily the sky
Is riv'n with angels singing;
    Gloria, hosanna in excelsis!
    Gloria, hosanna in excelsis!

E'ev so here below, below,
Let steeple bells be swungen.
And io, io, io
By priest and people sungen;
    Gloria, hosanna in excelsis!
    Gloria, hosanna in excelsis!

Pray you, dutifully prime
Your matin chime, ye ringers;
May you beautifully rime
Your evetime song, ye singers:
    Gloria, hosanna in excelsis!
    Gloria, hosanna in excelsis!

*Capo at third fret

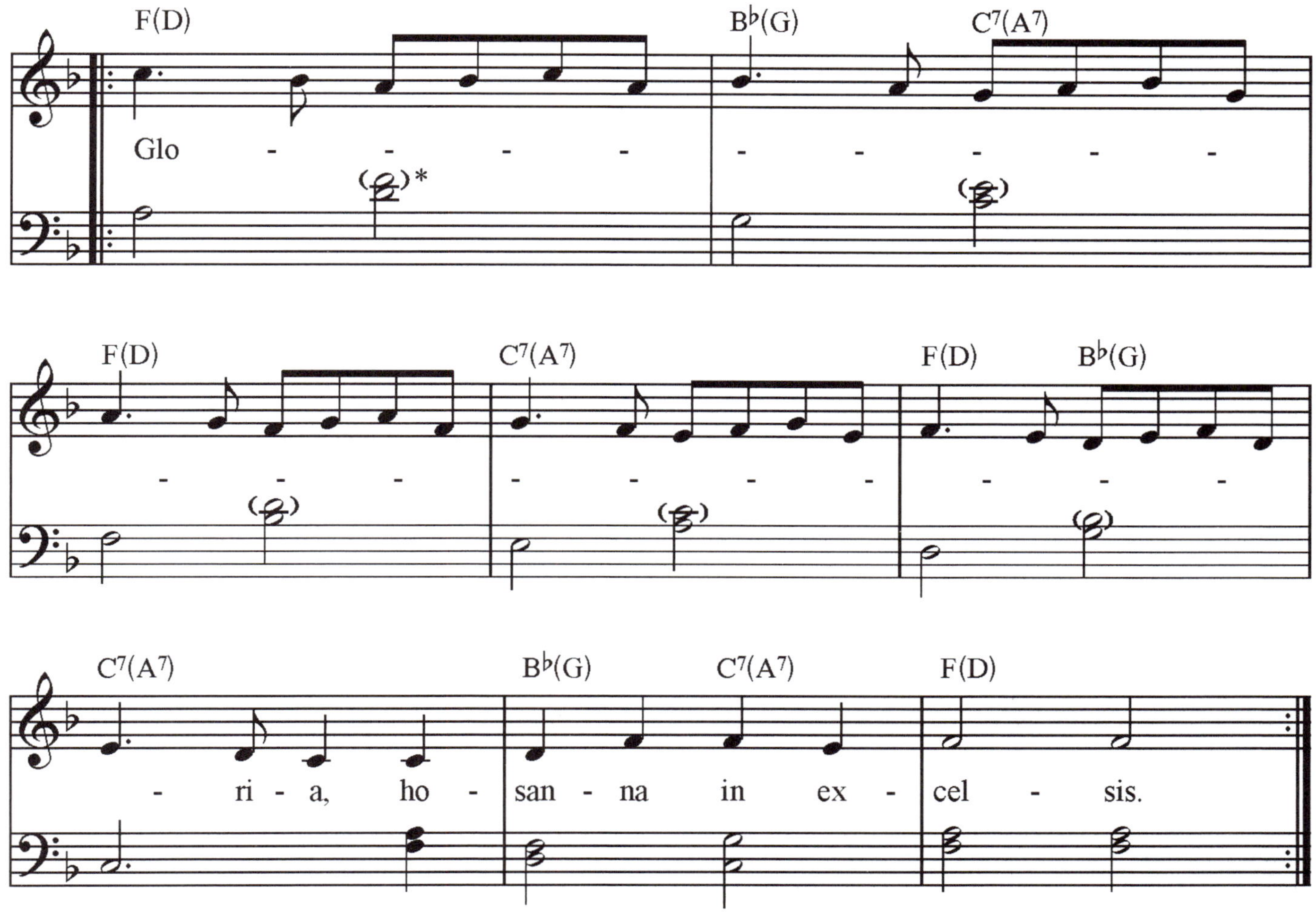

F(D) B♭(G) C⁷(A⁷)

Glo - - - - - - - - - -
(𝅘𝅥)*   (𝅘𝅥)

F(D) C⁷(A⁷) F(D) B♭(G)

- - - - - - - - -
(𝅘𝅥)   (𝅘𝅥)   (𝅘𝅥)

C⁷(A⁷) B♭(G) C⁷(A⁷) F(D)

- ri - a, ho - san - na in ex - cel - sis.

Activity: Can you see the little elf hiding on this page?

Hark! The herald angels sing

Hark! The herald angels sing
Glory to the new-born King;
Peace on earth and mercy mild,
God and sinners reconciled:
Joyful all ye nations rise,
Join the triumph of the skies,
With th'angelic host proclaim:
Christ is born in Bethlehem.
>Hark! The herald angels sing
>Glory to the new-born King.

Christ, by highest heaven adored,
Christ, the everlasting Lord,
Late in time behold him come,
Offspring of the virgin's womb:
Veiled in flesh the Godhead see,
Hail the incarnate Deity!
Pleased as Man with man to dwell,
Jesus, our Emmanuel.
>Hark! The herald angels sing
>Glory to the new-born King.

Hail, the heaven-born Prince of Peace!
Hail the Sun of Righteousness!
Light and life to all he brings,
Risen with healing in his wings.
Mild he lays his glory by,
Born that man no more may die,
Born to raise the sons of earth,
Born to give them second birth.
>Hark! The herald angels sing
>Glory to the new-born King.

*Capo at third fret

Activity: Colour the Christmas border.

C(A)   F(D)   C(A)   F(D)   C(A)   C(A)   F(D)   C(A)   F(D)   C(A)

Joy - ful   all   ye   na - tions   rise,____   Join   the   tri - umph   of   the   skies,____

B♭(G)   Cm(Am)   Gm(Em)   D(B)   Gm(Em)   C(A)   F(D)   C(A)   F(D)

With   th'an - ge - lic   host   pro - claim,   Christ   is____   born   in   Beth - le - hem:

B♭(G)   Cm(Am)   Gm(Em)   D(B)   Gm(Em)   C(A)   F(D)   C(A)   F(D)

Hark!   the   he - rald   an - gels   sing   Glo - ry____   to   the   new - born   King.

I saw three ships

I saw three ships come sailing in
> On Christmas Day, on Christmas Day,

I saw three ships come sailing in
> On Christmas Day in the morning.

And what was in those ships all three?
> On Christmas Day, on Christmas Day …

Our Saviour Christ and his lady,
> On Christmas Day, on Christmas Day …

Pray, whither sailed those ships all three?
> On Christmas Day, on Christmas Day …

Oh, they sailed into Bethlehem
> On Christmas Day, on Christmas Day …

And all the bells on earth shall ring
> On Christmas Day, on Christmas Day …

And all the angels in heaven shall sing
> On Christmas Day, on Christmas Day …

*Capo at third fret

1. I saw three ships come sailing in On Christmas Day, on Christmas Day, I saw three ships come sailing in On Christmas Day in the morning.

Activity: Colour the robins.

It came upon the midnight clear

It came upon the midnight clear,
That glorious song of old,
From angels bending near the earth
To touch their harps of gold:
'Peace on the earth, goodwill to men,
From heaven's all-gracious King!'
The world in solemn stillness lay
To hear the angels sing.

Yet with the woes of sin and strife
The world has suffered long;
Beneath the angel-strain have rolled
Two thousand years of wrong;
And man, at war with man, hears not
The love-song which they bring;
O hush the noise, ye men of strife,
And hear the angels sing.

For lo! The days are hastening on,
By prophet-bards foretold,
When, with the ever-circling years,
Comes round the age of gold;
When peace shall over all the earth
Its ancient splendours fling,
And the whole world give back the song
Which now the angels sing.

Activity: Colour the Christmas presents.
Add some angel stickers to this page.

Music for "It Came Upon the Midnight Clear"

1. It came up-on the midnight clear, That glo-rious song of old, From an-gels bend-ing near the earth To touch their harps of gold: 'Peace on the earth, good-will to men, From heav'n's all-gra-cious King!' The world in so-lemn still-ness lay To hear the an-gels sing.

Tuned percussion

Little Jesus, sweetly sleep

Little Jesus, sweetly sleep, do not stir;
We will lend a coat of fur.
We will rock you, rock you, rock you,
We will rock you, rock you, rock you:
See the fur to keep you warm,
Snugly round your tiny form.

Mary's little baby, sleep sweetly sleep,
Sleep in comfort, slumber deep.
We will rock you, rock you, rock you,
We will rock you, rock you, rock you:
We will serve you all we can,
Darling, darling little man.

Words: translated by Percy Dearmer (1867-1936)
Melody: traditional Czech carol collected by Martin Shaw (1875-1958)

1. Lit - tle Je - sus, sweet - ly ___ sleep, do not ___ stir;

We will ___ lend a ___ coat of ___ fur. We will rock you, rock you, rock you,

D   A   D

We will rock you, rock you, rock— you: See the fur to

Ddim⁷   A   G   D   A⁷   D

keep you— warm, Snug - ly— round your— ti - ny— form.

Activity: Add a
sticker reindeer,
robin and Santa
to the page.

15

O come, all ye faithful

O come, all ye faithful,
Joyful and triumphant,
O come ye, O come ye to
Bethlehem;
Come and behold him,
Born the King of angels.
O come let us adore him,
O come let us adore him,
O come let us adore him,
Christ the Lord!

God of God!
Light of light,
Lo! He abhors not the
Virgin's womb;
Very God,
Begotten not created.
O come let us adore him,
O come let us adore him,
O come let us adore him,
Christ the Lord!

Sing, choirs of angels,
Sing in exultation,
Sing, all ye citizens of
heaven above:
Glory to God
In the highest.
O come let us adore him,
O come let us adore him,
O come let us adore him,
Christ the Lord!

Yea, Lord, we greet thee,
Born this happy morning,
Jesu, to thee be glory given;
Word of the Father,
Now in flesh appearing:
O come let us adore him,
O come let us adore him,
O come let us adore him,
Christ the Lord!

*Capo at third fret

16

Page 2-3

Page 12-13

Page 14-15

Page 20-21

Page 28-29

come, let us a - dore him, O come, let us a - dore him, O

come, let us a - dore him,___ Christ___ the Lord!

Melody instruments

F(D)

C(A)

F(D) B♭(G) F(D) C(A) F(D)

Activity: Colour the Christmas border and the decorations.

O little town of Bethlehem

O little town of Bethlehem,
How still we see thee lie!
Above thy deep and dreamless sleep
The silent stars go by.
Yet in thy dark streets shineth
The everlasting light;
The hopes and fears of all the years
Are met in thee tonight.

O morning stars, together
Proclaim thy holy birth,
And praises sing to God the King,
And peace to men on earth;
For Christ is born of Mary;
And, gathered all above.
While mortals sleep the angels keep
Their watch of wondering love.

How silently, how silently
The wondrous gift is given!
So God imparts to human hearts
The blessings of his heaven.
No ear may hear his coming,
But in this world of sin
Where meek souls will receive him, still
The dear Christ enters in.

Where children pure and happy
Pray to the blessèd Child,
Where misery cries out to thee,
Son of the mother mild;
Where charity stands watching
And faith holds wide the door,
The dark night wakes, the glory breaks,
And Christmas comes once more.

O holy child of Bethlehem,
Descend to us, we pray;
Cast out our sin and enter in,
Be born in us today.
We hear the Christmas angels
The great glad tidings tell:
O come to us, abide with us.
Our Lord Emmanuel.

Words: Bishop Philips Brooks (1835-93)
Melody: 'Forest Green', traditional English tune
adapted by R. Vaughan Williams (1872-1958)

*Capo at third fret

Activity: Match the Christmas stocking to each house. The clue is in the colours.

Silent night

Silent night, holy night!
All is calm, all is bright
Round yon virgin mother and child.
Holy infant so tender and mild,
Sleep in heavenly peace,
Sleep in heavenly peace.

Silent night, holy night!
Shepherds quake at the sight:
Glories stream from heaven afar,
Heavenly hosts sing: Alleluia,
Christ the Saviour is born!
Christ the Saviour is born!

Sllent night, holy night!
Son of God, love's pure light,
Radiance beams from thy holy face
With the dawn of redeeming grace,
Jesus, Lord at thy birth,
Jesus, Lord at thy birth.

*Capo at second fret

Ho - ly in - fant so ten - der and mild, Sleep in hea - ven - ly peace,____ Sleep__ in hea - ven - ly peace.

D(C) A(G) Bm(Am) E⁷(D⁷) F♯(Em) A(G) E⁷(D⁷) A(G)

Activity: Add sticker lights to complete the border.

The first Nowell

The first Nowell the angel did say
Was to certain poor shepherds in fields as they lay;
In fields where they lay, keeping their sheep,
On a cold winter's night that was so deep:
    Nowell, Nowell, Nowell, Nowell,
    Born is the King of Israel.

They looked up and saw a star
Shining in the east, beyond them far.
And to the earth it gave great light,
And so it continued both day and night:
    Nowell, Nowell, Nowell, Nowell …

And by the light of that same star,
Three wise men came from country far.
To seek for a King was their intent,
And to follow the star wheresoever it went:
    Nowell, Nowell, Nowell, Nowell …

This star drew nigh to the north-west;
O'er Bethlehem it took its rest,
And there it did both stop and stay
Right over the place where Jesus lay:
    Nowell, Nowell, Nowell, Nowell …

Then entered in those wise men three,
Fell reverently upon their knee,
And offered there in his presence
Both gold and myrrh and frankincense:
    Nowell, Nowell, Nowell, Nowell …

Then let us all with one accord
Sing praises to our heavenly Lord,
Who hath made heaven and earth of naught,
And with his blood mankind hath bought:
    Nowell, Nowell, Nowell, Nowell …

fields___ where___ they lay,___ keep-ing their sheep, On a
cold win-ter's night___ that was___ so deep: No-
-well___ No-well, No-well, No-well,
Born is the King___ of Is - ra - el.

Activity: Colour the Christmas
gifts in the border.

The holly and the ivy

The holly and the ivy,
When they are both full grown,
Of all the trees that are in the wood
The holly bears the crown:
    O the rising of the sun
    And the running of the deer,
    The playing of the merry organ,
    Sweet singing in the choir.

The holly bears a blossom
As white as any flower,
And Mary bore sweet Jesus Christ
To be our sweet Saviour:
    O the rising of the sun …

The holly bears a berry
As red as any blood,
And Mary bore sweet Jesus Christ
To do poor sinners good:
    O the rising of the sun …

Repeat first verse.

Activity: Colour the Christmas stockings.
Add sticker holly to the border.

While shepherds watched

While shepherds watched their flocks by night,
All seated on the ground,
The angel of the Lord came down
And glory shone around.

'Fear not,' said he, for mighty dread
Had seized their troubled mind;
'Glad tidings of great joy I bring
To you and all mankind.

'To you in David's town this day
Is born of David's line
A Saviour, who is Christ the Lord,
And this shall be the sign:

'The heavenly babe you there shall find
To human view displayed,
All meanly wrapped in swathing bands,
And in a manger laid.'

Thus spoke the seraph, and forthwith
Appeared a shining throng
Of angels praising God, who thus
Addresses their joyful song:

'All glory be to God on high,
And to the earth be peace,
Goodwill henceforth from heaven to men
Begin and never cease.'

Activity: Colour the
Christmas border and
add stickers to the page.

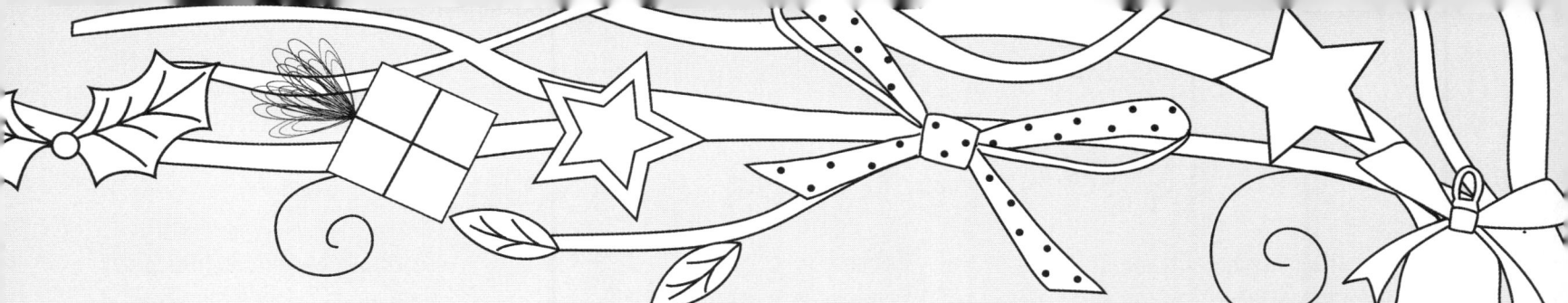
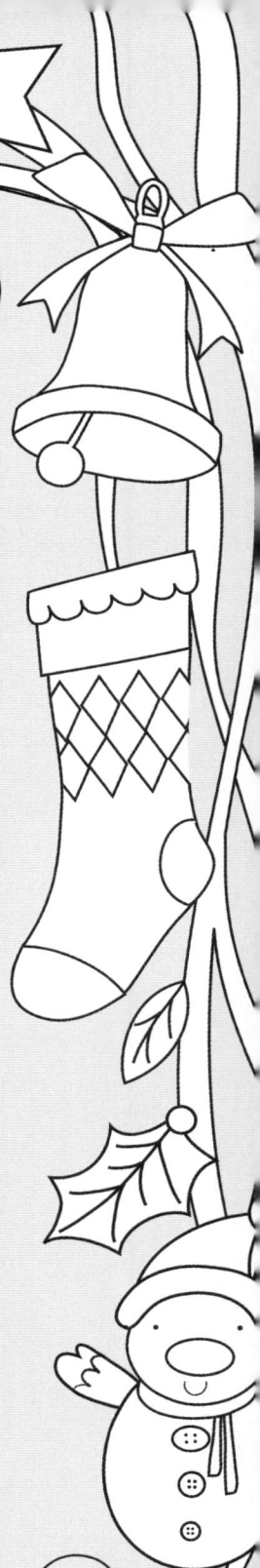

D   G   D

1. While   shep   -   herds watched their   flocks   by   night,   All

D   D   D   G   D

Tenor recorders or tuned percussion

       E^7 A   D   G   D

seat   -   ed   on   the   ground,   The   an   -   gel   of   the

D   E   A   D   G   G   D

A   D   Em A^7 D

Lord   came   down   And   glo   -   ry   shone   a   -   round.

A   A   G   A   D

We three kings of Orient are

We three kings of Orient are;
Bearing gifts we traverse afar,
Field and fountain, moor and mountain,
Following yonder star.
O star of wonder, star of night,
Star with royal beauty bright,
Westward leading, still proceeding,
Guide us to thy perfect light.

Melchior:

Born a king on Bethlehem's plain,
Gold l bring to crown him again
King for ever, ceasing never
Over us all to reign.
O star of wonder, star of night …

Caspar:

Frankincense to offer have l,
Incense owns a Deity nigh.
Prayer and praising, all men raising,
Worship him, God most high.
O star of wonder, star of night …

Balthazar:

Myrrh is mine; its bitter perfume
Breathes a life of gathering gloom.
Sorrowing, sighing, bleeding, dying,
Sealed in the stone-cold tomb.
O star of wonder, star of night …

Glorious now behold him arise,
King, and God, and sacrifice!
Heaven sings alleluia,
Alleluia the earth replies
O star of wonder, star of night,
Star with royal beauty bright,
Westward leading, still proceeding,
Guide us to thy perfect light.

Activity: Colour the kings and add sticker hats to the border.

28

Chorus

Gm	A⁷	Dm	C

Fol - low - ing yon - der star. O_____

G · A · D · C

F	B♭	F

star of won - der, star of night,

F · F · B♭ · F

B♭	F

Star with roy - al beau - ty bright,

F · F · B♭ · F

Dm	C	B♭	C

West - ward lead - ing, still pro - ceed - ing,

D · C · B♭ · C

F	B♭	F

Guide us to thy per - fect light.

F · F · B♭ · F

29

We wish you a merry Christmas

We wish you a merry Christmas,
We wish you a merry Christmas,
We wish you a merry Christmas,
And a happy New Year.
    Good tidings we bring
    To you and your kin,
    We wish you a merry Christmas
    And a happy New Year.

Now bring us some figgy pudding,
Now bring us some figgy pudding,
Now bring us some figgy pudding,
And bring some out here.
    Good tidings we bring
    To you and your kin,
    We wish you a merry Christmas
    And a happy New Year.

And we won't go until we've got some,
And we won't go until we've got some,
And we won't go until we've got some,
So bring some out here.
    Good tidings we bring
    To you and your kin,
    We wish you a merry Christmas
    And a happy New Year.

Activity: Colour the Christmas stamps and
design your own.

We Wish You a Merry Christmas

1. We wish you a merry Christ-mas, We wish you a merry Christ-mas, We wish you a mer-ry Christ-mas, And a hap-py New Year. Good tid-ings we bring To you and your kin, We wish you a mer-ry Christ-mas And a hap-py New Year.

Tuned percussion chords: G C A D B E C D G G D G A D G B C D G

Add stickers to the boxes when you have learned the carols in this book.

Away in a manger	☐	O little town of Bethlehem	☐
Angels from the realms of glory	☐	Silent night	☐
Ding dong merrily on high	☐	The first Nowell	☐
Hark! The herald angels sing	☐	The holly and the ivy	☐
I saw three ships	☐	While shepherds watched	☐
It came upon the midnight clear	☐	We three kings of Orient are	☐
Little Jesus, sweetly sleep	☐	We wish you a merry Christmas	☐
O come, all ye faithful	☐		

Acknowledgements
For the following traditional songs, piano accompaniments are by Timothy Roberts and music is by Jeanne Roberts.
Originally published in Sing Nowell © 1989 A&C Black Publishers Ltd, an imprint of Bloomsbury Publishing Plc. Reproduced by permission. All rights reserved.
'Away in a manger' words: anon., melody: W. J. Kirkpatrick (1838–1921)
'Angels from the realms of glory' words: James Montgomery (1771–1854), melody: traditional French tune
'Ding dong merrily on high' words: G. R. Woodward (1848–1934), melody: 'Branche de l'Official' from Thornton Arbeau's Orchesographie (1588)
'Hark! The herald angels sing' words: Charles Wesley (1707–1788), melody: F. Mendelssohn-Bartholdy (1809–1847)
'I saw three ships' words and melody: traditional English
'It came upon the midnight clear' words: E. H. Sears (1810–1876), melody: traditional English adapted by Arthur Sullivan (1842–1900)
'O come, all ye faithful' words: translated from the Latin by F. Oakley (1802–1880), melody: 'Adeste Fideles', 18th century Latin hymn
'Silent night' words: Joseph Mohr (1792–1848), translator anon., melody: Franz Gruber (1787–1863)
'The first Nowell' words and melody: traditional English
'The holly and the ivy' words and melody: traditional English, collected by Cecil Sharp (1859–1924)
'While shepherds watched' words: Nahum Tate (1652–1715), melody: 'Winchester Old' from Este's Psalter (1852)
'We three kings of Orient are' words and melody: J. H. Hopkins (1820–1891)
'We wish you a merry Christmas' words and melody: English traditional

Grateful acknowledgement is made to Oxford University Press for permission to use the following:
'Little Jesus, sweetly sleep' melody collected by Martin Shaw, from The Oxford Book of Carols © 1928
'O little town of Bethlehem' melody (Forest Green) collected and arranged by R. Vaughan Williams (1872–1958), from The English Hymnal © 1906